CONTENTS

Understanding the MAP Tests 3

Purpose and Benefits of MAP Testing 4

Test Format and Content.. 4

Adaptive Testing and Scoring System 5

Preparing for Success on the MAP Test... 5

What Is Contained Within this Book? 6

Topic 1 – Definitions... 7

Topic 1 - Answers 17

Topic 2 – Identifying Genres... 19

Topic 2 - Answers 29

Topic 3 – Homonyms and Homophones... 31

Topic 3 - Answers 41

Topic 4 – Story Elements 43

Topic 4 - Answers 57

Topic 5 – Points of View 56

Topic 5 - Answers 65

Topic 6 – Summarizing Texts 67

Topic 6 - Answers 79

Topic 7 – Synonyms and Antonyms 81

Topic 7 – Answers 91

Topic 8 – Understanding Mood 93

Topic 8 – Answers 105

Ready for More? 107

Understanding the MAP Tests

The NWEA MAP (Measures of Academic Progress) test is an adaptive assessment that is designed to measure student growth and progress in a variety of subject areas. The test is taken by millions of students across the United States and is widely used by educators to help inform instruction and measure student outcomes. The NWEA MAP test is administered online and provides immediate feedback on student performance, allowing teachers to adjust their teaching strategies and provide targeted support to individual students.

The NWEA MAP test is unique in that it is adaptive, which means that the difficulty of the questions adjusts based on the student's responses. This allows the test to be more personalized to each student's abilities and provides a more accurate measure of their knowledge and skills. The test covers a range of subject areas, including mathematics, reading, language usage, and science, and is administered multiple times throughout the school year. This allows teachers to track student progress and growth over time and make data-driven decisions to improve student outcomes.

Purpose and Benefits of MAP Testing

The primary purpose of the MAP Test is to provide valuable insights into a student's learning and academic progress. By offering a detailed analysis of a student's performance in reading, language usage, mathematics, and science, the test helps teachers tailor their instruction to meet individual needs. The MAP Test also serves as a benchmarking tool, allowing schools and districts to compare their students' performance with national norms and other local institutions.

This data-driven approach enables educators to make informed decisions about curriculum, instructional methods, and resource allocation, ultimately leading to improved student outcomes. Additionally, the MAP Test can help identify gifted students who may benefit from advanced or accelerated programs, as well as students who may require additional support or interventions.

Test Format and Content

The MAP Test is divided into four primary content areas: reading, language usage, mathematics, and science. Each section consists of multiple-choice questions that cover various topics and skills within the respective subject. The test is untimed, allowing students to work at their own pace and ensuring a lower level of test anxiety. The computer-adaptive nature of the MAP Test ensures that the difficulty of questions adjusts based on a student's performance, making it suitable for students of all ability levels. As a result, the MAP Test not only evaluates a student's mastery of grade-level content but also assesses their readiness for more advanced material.

Adaptive Testing and Scoring System

One of the unique aspects of the MAP Test is its adaptive testing system. As students answer questions, the test adjusts the difficulty of subsequent questions based on their performance. This adaptive nature allows the test to home in on a student's true ability level, providing more accurate and meaningful results. The MAP Test uses a RIT (Rasch Unit) scale to measure student achievement, which is an equal-interval scale that allows for easy comparison of scores across grade levels and subjects. This scoring system allows educators and parents to track a student's growth over time, making it an invaluable tool for understanding academic progress and setting individualized learning goals.

Preparing for Success on the MAP Test

Effective preparation for the MAP Test involves a combination of understanding the test format, mastering content knowledge, and developing test-taking strategies. This test prep book is designed to provide students with comprehensive guidance on each content area, offering targeted instruction and practice questions to build confidence and ensure success. Additionally, the book includes test-taking tips and strategies to help students approach the test with a calm and focused mindset. By working through this book and dedicating time to consistent practice, students will be well-equipped to excel on the MAP Test and achieve their academic goals.

Note that, since there is no cap to the level that a student can work to in preparation for this test, there is no 'completion' of content, as students can simply do questions from grades above in preparation. It should be noted that students are not expected to work far above grade level to succeed in this test, as consistent correct answers are more relevant.

What Is Contained Within this Book?

Within this book you will find 320 questions based off content which would be found within the MAP test your student will take. The content found in this book will be the equivalent of grade 3 level. Note that since this test is adaptive, some students may benefit by looking at several grade levels of content, not just their own.

At the end of the book will contain answers alongside explanations. It is recommended to look and check your answers thoroughly in regular intervals to make sure you improve as similar questions come up.

Number	Topic Name	Questions	Answers
1	Definitions	p7	p17
2	Identifying Genres	P19	P29
3	Homonyms and Homophones	P31	P41
4	Story Elements	P43	P53
5	Points of View	P56	P65
6	Summarizing Texts	P67	P79
7	Synonyms and Antonyms	P81	P91
8	Understanding Mood	P93	P105

Topic 1 – Definitions

1.1) What does the word 'swift' mean?

☐ Very heavy

☐ Very fast

☐ Very slow

☐ Very loud

1.2) How would you describe something that is 'fragile'?

☐ Very strong

☐ Extremely heavy

☐ Very soft

☐ Easily broken or damaged

1.3) What does 'harvest' mean?

☐ Playing in the garden

☐ Planting seeds

☐ Cooking food

☐ Gathering crops from fields

1.4) What is a 'festival'?

☐ A type of music

☐ A book title

☐ A celebration or event

☐ A kind of food

1.5) How would you describe 'enormous'?

☐ Something very cold

☐ Something very small

☐ Something very large

☐ Something very light

1.6) What does 'delicate' mean?

☐ Easily broken or damaged

☐ Extremely heavy

☐ Very fast

☐ Very strong

1.7) What is 'humidity'?

☐ Coldness in the air

☐ Dryness in the air

☐ Heat in the air

☐ Moisture in the air

1.8) What does 'invent' mean?

☐ To remember something old

☐ To travel somewhere

☐ To create something new

☐ To buy something

1.9) How would you describe 'jovial'?

☐ Serious and strict

☐ Sad and gloomy

☐ Cheerful and friendly

☐ Quiet and shy

1.10) What does 'knead' mean in cooking?

☐ To slice dough

☐ To freeze dough

☐ To cook dough

☐ To mix dough with hands

1.11) What does 'nimble' mean?

☐ Slow

☐ Loud

☐ Heavy

☐ Quick and light in movement

1.12) How would you describe an 'ornate' object?

☐ Decorated in a complex way

☐ Invisible

☐ Soft

☐ Plain

1.13) What is 'parched'?

☐ Hot

☐ Extremely dry

☐ Very wet

☐ Cold

1.14) What does 'quaint' mean?

☐ Fast

☐ Loud

☐ Modern

☐ Charming and old-fashioned

1.15) How would you describe 'rugged' terrain?

☐ Uneven and tough

☐ Soft

☐ Slippery

☐ Smooth and flat

1.16) What does 'seldom' mean?

☐ Loudly

☐ Quickly

☐ Always

☐ Not often

1.17) What is a 'tranquil' place like?

☐ Loud and busy

☐ Cold

☐ Bright

☐ Calm and peaceful

1.18) How would you describe something 'unique'?

☐ Unimportant

☐ Common

☐ Being the only one of its kind

☐ Boring

1.19) What does 'vast' refer to?

☐ Heavy

☐ Very large in size

☐ Light

☐ Small

1.20) What is 'weary' used to describe?

☐ Tired or exhausted

☐ Cold

☐ Happy

☐ Energetic

1.21) What does 'zestful' mean?

- ☐ Slow
- ☐ Quiet
- ☐ Sad
- ☐ Energetic

1.22) How would you describe a 'yawning' gap?

- ☐ Narrow
- ☐ Closed
- ☐ Very wide or large
- ☐ Small

1.23) What is 'xenial' hospitality?

- ☐ Scary
- ☐ Loud
- ☐ Friendly towards strangers
- ☐ Unwelcoming

1.24) What does 'wistful' mean?

- ☐ Happy
- ☐ Angry
- ☐ Thoughtful and longing
- ☐ Loud

1.25) How would you describe 'vibrant' colors?

☐ Light

☐ Bright and full of life

☐ Dark

☐ Dull

1.26) What does 'uproarious' laughter sound like?

☐ Angry

☐ Sad

☐ Very loud and funny

☐ Quiet

1.27) What is a 'tranquil' place like?

☐ Cold

☐ Calm and peaceful

☐ Loud and busy

☐ Bright

1.28) How would you describe something 'serene'?

☐ Calm and peaceful

☐ Angry

☐ Colorful

☐ Loud

1.29) What does 'quizzical' expression show?

☐ Curious or puzzled

☐ Angry

☐ Scared

☐ Happy

1.30) What is 'pristine' used to describe?

☐ Perfectly clean and untouched

☐ Noisy

☐ Old

☐ Dirty

1.31) What does 'jubilant' mean?

☐ Quiet

☐ Angry

☐ Sad

☐ Very happy and excited

1.32) How would you describe something 'luminous'?

☐ Glowing or shining

☐ Dull

☐ Loud

☐ Heavy

1.33) What is 'melancholy'?

☐ Noisy

☐ Happy

☐ Colorful

☐ Sad and thoughtful

1.34) What does 'nostalgic' mean?

☐ Worried about the future

☐ Feeling happy about the past

☐ Thinking about the present

☐ No feelings

1.35) How would you describe 'opulent'?

☐ Boring

☐ Common

☐ Rich and luxurious

☐ Poor and simple

1.36) What does 'placid' mean?

☐ Cold and icy

☐ Loud and noisy

☐ Calm and peaceful

☐ Fast and exciting

1.37) What does it mean if a king 'abdicates'?

☐ He becomes king

☐ He leaves the throne

☐ He makes someone a knight

☐ He puts on his crown

1.38) How would you describe something 'robust'?

☐ Strong and healthy

☐ Weak

☐ Quiet

☐ Slow

1.39) What does 'merchandise' mean?

☐ Something you buy or sell

☐ Something that is cold

☐ Something that you roll for board games

☐ Something that you wear

1.40) How would you describe 'turbulent' weather?

☐ Cold

☐ Stormy and rough

☐ Sunny

☐ Calm

Topic 1 – Answers

Question Number	Answer	Explanation
1.1	Very fast	'Swift' means moving or capable of moving at high speed.
1.2	Easily broken or damaged	Something 'fragile' is not strong or sturdy and can break easily.
1.3	Gathering crops from fields	'Harvest' is the process of gathering mature crops from the fields.
1.4	A celebration or event	A 'festival' is an event or series of events, usually celebrating something.
1.5	Something very large	'Enormous' refers to something very large in size or extent.
1.6	Easily broken or damaged	'Delicate' means something that is fine in texture and easily damaged.
1.7	Moisture in the air	'Humidity' refers to the amount of moisture present in the air.
1.8	To create something new	To 'invent' means to come up with or create something that did not exist before.
1.9	Cheerful and friendly	'Jovial' describes someone who is cheerful and friendly.
1.10	To mix dough with hands	'Knead' in cooking means to work and press dough with the hands.
1.11	Quick and light in movement	'Nimble' means moving quickly and easily; agile.
1.12	Decorated in a complex way	'Ornate' refers to something decorated elaborately or excessively.
1.13	Extremely dry	'Parched' means extremely dry or thirsty.
1.14	Charming and old-fashioned	'Quaint' is used to describe something attractively unusual or old-fashioned.
1.15	Uneven and tough	'Rugged' terrain is rough, irregular, and uneven.
1.16	Not often	'Seldom' means not often or rarely.
1.17	Calm and peaceful	A 'tranquil' place is quiet and peaceful.
1.18	Being the only one of its kind	'Unique' means being the only one of its kind; unlike anything else.

1.19	Very large in size	'Vast' refers to something very large in size, extent, or quantity.
1.20	Tired or exhausted	'Weary' is used to describe feeling tired or exhausted.
1.21	Full of energy and enthusiasm	'Zestful' means full of energy, enthusiasm, or eagerness.
1.22	Very wide or large	A 'yawning' gap is very wide, large, or extensive.
1.23	Friendly towards strangers	'Xenial' hospitality refers to being friendly and welcoming towards strangers.
1.24	Thoughtful and longing	'Wistful' indicates a feeling of vague or regretful longing.
1.25	Bright and full of life	'Vibrant' colors are bright, vivid, and full of life.
1.26	Very loud and funny	'Uproarious' laughter is very loud and boisterous, often funny.
1.27	Calm and peaceful	A 'tranquil' place is characterized by calmness and peacefulness.
1.28	Calm and peaceful	Something 'serene' is calm, peaceful, and untroubled.
1.29	Curious or puzzled	A 'quizzical' expression shows that someone is puzzled or questioning.
1.30	Perfectly clean and untouched	'Pristine' describes something in its original condition; unspoiled.
1.31	Very happy and excited	'Jubilant' means feeling or expressing great happiness and triumph.
1.32	Glowing or shining	'Luminous' describes something that gives off light; glowing or shining.
1.33	Sad and thoughtful	'Melancholy' is a feeling of pensive sadness, typically with no obvious cause.
1.34	Feeling happy about the past	'Nostalgic' means having a sentimental longing for the past.
1.35	Rich and luxurious	'Opulent' describes something luxurious or rich, often lavish or ostentatious.
1.36	Calm and peaceful	'Placid' means not easily upset or excited; calm and peaceful.
1.37	He leaves the throne	'Abdicate' is when a monarch leaves the throne to the next in line.
1.38	Strong and healthy	Something 'robust' is strong, healthy, and vigorous.
1.39	Something that you buy or sell	'Merchandise' is a word to describe things you buy in a shop, which can be anything from food to clothes.
1.40	Stormy and rough	'Turbulent' weather is characterized by conflict, disorder, or confusion; not calm.

Topic 2 – Identifying Genres

2.1) What is a fairy tale usually about?

☐ Future technology

☐ Only real events

☐ Daily routines

☐ Magical characters and events

2.2) How can you tell if a book is realistic fiction?

☐ Tells the future

☐ Only about animals

☐ It seems real but is made up

☐ It's a true story

2.3) What does non-fiction mean?

☐ Made-up stories

☐ Jokes and riddles

☐ True information and facts

☐ Magical tales

2.4) What are the main elements of a fantasy story?

☐ Real life events

☐ Historical facts

☐ Everyday life

☐ Magic, imaginary worlds

2.5) What kind of book tells you facts about real things?

☐ Non-fiction book

☐ Fantasy

☐ Fairy tale

☐ Comic book

2.6) Can fairy tales have magical elements?

☐ Only in movies

☐ No, never

☐ Yes, often

☐ Only in comics

2.7) What does 'biography' mean?

☐ A story of someone's life

☐ An animal story

☐ A space story

☐ A magical story

2.8) How can you tell a story is a myth?

☐ Real life stories

☐ School life

☐ Future stories

☐ Ancient stories, often with gods

2.9) What type of story could be about animals that talk?

☐ Textbook

☐ Non-fiction

☐ Fantasy or fairy tale

☐ Biography

2.10) How is historical fiction different from a history book?

☐ No difference

☐ Only for adults

☐ Historical fiction has made-up stories in real settings

☐ Only about wars

2.11) What kind of story has a moral at the end?

☐ Biography

☐ Fantasy

☐ Comic book

☐ Fable

2.12) What does an autobiography tell you about?

☐ History of a place

☐ Another person's life

☐ Fictional story

☐ Someone's own life story

2.13) Are comic books considered a genre?

☐ Only for adults

☐ Yes, with unique storytelling

☐ Only about sports

☐ No, not a genre

2.14) What does 'science fiction' involve?

☐ Magical creatures

☐ Future, advanced technology

☐ Present events

☐ Past events

2.15) Can a non-fiction book be about dinosaurs?

☐ Only about birds

☐ No, only fictional animals

☐ Yes, about extinct animals

☐ Only about pets

2.16) How do adventure stories usually make you feel?

☐ Sad

☐ Scared

☐ Bored

☐ Excited and curious

2.17) What is a genre of a book with lots of facts and real information?

☐ Fantasy

☐ Fairy tale

☐ Mystery

☐ Non-fiction

2.18) Can a biography be about someone who is still alive?

☐ Only about fictional characters

☐ No

☐ Yes

☐ Only about ancient people

2.19) What genre often has magic wands and witches?

☐ Fantasy

☐ Non-fiction

☐ Historical fiction

☐ Realistic fiction

2.20) What is the main purpose of a science fiction book?

☐ To tell true stories

☐ To explore imagined future or technology

☐ To make you laugh

☐ To teach history

2.21) What genre would include a story about a long-ago kingdom?

☐ Science fiction

☐ Historical fiction

☐ Biography

☐ Non-fiction

2.22) What type of book is a guide to different types of rocks?

☐ Fantasy

☐ Mystery

☐ Non-fiction

☐ Fairy tale

2.23) What might you find in a realistic fiction book?

☐ Ancient history

☐ Space adventures

☐ Everyday life situations

☐ Magical events

2.24) What kind of book is about animals and their habitats?

☐ Mystery

☐ Fantasy

☐ Fairy tale

☐ Non-fiction

2.25) What genre tells stories through pictures and dialogue?

☐ Non-fiction

☐ Graphic novel

☐ Biography

☐ Poetry

2.26) What kind of book would have a lot of jokes and funny stories?

☐ Comedy

☐ Historical fiction

☐ Non-fiction

☐ Fairy tale

2.27) What type of story has a hero who goes on a quest?

☐ Adventure

☐ Biography

☐ Non-fiction

☐ Realistic fiction

2.28) Can a book of poems belong to a specific genre?

☐ Yes, such as Haiku

☐ No, never

☐ Only when it has a problem to solve

☐ Only in fiction

2.29) How is a play different from a novel?

☐ No difference

☐ Performed with actors, novel is written text

☐ Novels are shorter

☐ Plays are always non-fiction

2.30) What genre would a book about space exploration be?

☐ Non-fiction or science fiction

☐ Mystery

☐ Fantasy

☐ Historical fiction

2.31) What genre is a story about a magical kingdom?

☐ Realistic fiction

☐ Non-fiction

☐ Fantasy

☐ Biography

2.32) What type of book would explain how volcanoes work?

☐ Comedy

☐ Fairy tale

☐ Fantasy

☐ Non-fiction

2.33) What might you find in a science fiction book?

☐ Aliens, futuristic technology

☐ Real-life stories

☐ Animal characters

☐ Historical events

2.34) What is the genre of a book about famous painters?

☐ Biography or non-fiction

☐ Mystery

☐ Adventure

☐ Fantasy

2.35) What kind of story usually has animals as the main characters?

☐ Science fiction

☐ Non-fiction

☐ Fable or folk tale

☐ Biography

2.36) What genre includes books about space and planets?

☐ Comedy

☐ Historical fiction

☐ Non-fiction or science fiction

☐ Fantasy

2.37) What type of book tells stories about ancient gods and goddesses?

☐ Realistic fiction

☐ Mythology

☐ Non-fiction

☐ Science fiction

2.38) How can you tell if a book is a mystery?

☐ It has magic

☐ It's about school

☐ It has a mystery or problem to solve

☐ It's about real events

2.39) What genre would a book about a child's school life be?

☐ Science fiction

☐ Fantasy

☐ Mythology

☐ Realistic fiction

2.40) What type of book would have recipes and cooking tips?

☐ Adventure

☐ Cookbook

☐ Fairy tale

☐ Science book

Topic 2 - Answers

Question Number	Answer	Explanation
2.1	Magical characters and events	Fairy tales typically include magical elements and enchanting characters.
2.2	It seems real but is made up	Realistic fiction mirrors real life but is fabricated by the author.
2.3	True information and facts	Non-fiction books are based on factual information and real events.
2.4	Magic, imaginary worlds	Fantasy stories often include magic and imaginary worlds or creatures.
2.5	Non-fiction book	Non-fiction books provide factual information on real-life subjects.
2.6	Yes, often	Fairy tales commonly feature magical and fantastical elements.
2.7	A story of someone's life	Biographies narrate the life story of a person, often in detail.
2.8	Ancient stories, often with gods	Myths are traditional stories, often involving gods or legendary figures.
2.9	Fantasy or fairy tale	These genres frequently feature talking animals in their narratives.
2.10	Historical fiction has made-up stories in real settings	Historical fiction weaves fictional tales within real historical settings.
2.11	Fable	Fables are short stories that typically convey a moral or lesson.
2.12	Someone's own life story	An autobiography is a person's life story written by themselves.
2.13	Yes, with unique storytelling	Comic books, with their distinctive format, constitute a literary genre.
2.14	Future, advanced technology	Science fiction explores futuristic concepts and advanced technology.
2.15	Yes, about extinct animals	Non-fiction books about dinosaurs provide factual information on these extinct creatures.
2.16	Excited and curious	Adventure stories are designed to evoke excitement and curiosity.
2.17	Non-fiction	Non-fiction books are characterized by factual and real information.
2.18	Yes	Biographies can be written about individuals who are still living.
2.19	Fantasy	Fantasy stories often include elements like magic wands and witches.
2.20	To explore imagined future or technology	Science fiction explores speculative and imaginative future scenarios.

2.21	Historical fiction	This genre features stories set in past eras, often with a historical backdrop.
2.22	Non-fiction	Non-fiction books provide factual information, such as guides on various topics.
2.23	Everyday life situations	Realistic fiction depicts situations that could occur in everyday life.
2.24	Non-fiction	Non-fiction books about animals discuss real-life facts about animal life and habitats.
2.25	Graphic novel	Graphic novels tell stories primarily through illustrations and dialogue.
2.26	Comedy	Comedy books are filled with jokes and humorous stories.
2.27	Adventure	Adventure stories typically involve a hero on a quest or journey.
2.28	Yes, in poetry genres like haiku	Poetry can belong to specific genres, like haiku, which have distinct styles.
2.29	Performed with actors, novel is written text	Plays are scripted for performance, while novels are written narratives.
2.30	Non-fiction or science fiction	Books about space exploration can be factual (non-fiction) or speculative (science fiction).
2.31	Fantasy	Fantasy genre typically includes stories about magical kingdoms.
2.32	Non-fiction	Non-fiction books provide factual information, such as explaining natural phenomena.
2.33	Aliens, futuristic technology	Science fiction often includes elements like aliens and advanced technology.
2.34	Biography or non-fiction	Books about famous painters can be biographical or general non-fiction.
2.35	Fable or folk tale	Fables and folk tales often feature animals as main characters.
2.36	Non-fiction or science fiction	Books about space and planets can be factual or speculative in nature.
2.37	Mythology	Mythological stories often narrate tales about ancient gods and goddesses
2.38	It has a mystery or problem to solve	Mystery genre involves stories with puzzles or mysteries to be solved.
2.39	Realistic fiction	Realistic fiction could include everyday stories like a child's school life.
2.40	Cookbook	Cookbooks offer recipes and cooking tips.

Topic 3 - Homonyms and Homophones

3.1) What is the difference between 'flower' and 'flour'?

☐ 'Flower' is a color, 'flour' is for baking

☐ 'Flower' is a plant, 'flour' is ground wheat

☐ 'Flower' is an animal, 'flour' is a drink

☐ 'Flower' and 'flour' are the same

3.2) Choose the correct meaning of 'sea' and 'see'.

☐ 'Sea' is a sound, 'see' is a color

☐ 'Sea' is a food, 'see' is a drink

☐ 'Sea' is a large body of water, 'see' means to look

☐ 'Sea' and 'see' are the same

3.3) How are 'sun' and 'son' different?

☐ 'Sun' is a color, 'son' is a toy

☐ 'Sun' is a star, 'son' is a male child

☐ 'Sun' is a fruit, 'son' is a game

☐ 'Sun' and 'son' are the same

3.4) What does the homophone 'pair' mean compared to 'pear'?

☐ 'Pair' and 'pear' are the same

☐ 'Pair' is an animal, 'pear' is a toy

☐ 'Pair' means two of something, 'pear' is a fruit

☐ 'Pair' is a color, 'pear' is a drink

3.5) Explain the difference between 'mail' and 'male'.

☐ 'Mail' is an animal, 'male' is a drink

☐ 'Mail' is a color, 'male' is a food

☐ 'Mail' is letters and packages, 'male' is a gender

☐ 'Mail' and 'male' are the same

3.6) How do 'night' and 'knight' differ in meaning?

☐ 'Night' is a color, 'knight' is a toy

☐ 'Night' is a food, 'knight' is a drink

☐ 'Night' and 'knight' are the same

☐ 'Night' is when it's dark, 'knight' is a warrior

3.7) What is the difference between 'blue' and 'blew'?

☐ 'Blue' and 'blew' are the same

☐ 'Blue' is a fruit, 'blew' is a drink

☐ 'Blue' is a color, 'blew' means to blow air

☐ 'Blue' is a toy, 'blew' is a game

3.8) Compare the meanings of 'hair' and 'hare'.

☐ 'Hair' is a fruit, 'hare' is a drink

☐ 'Hair' and 'hare' are the same

☐ 'Hair' is a color, 'hare' is a food

☐ 'Hair' is on your head, 'hare' is an animal

3.9) What is the difference between 'tail' and 'tale'?

☐ 'Tail' is a color, 'tale' is a food

☐ 'Tail' is the end of an animal, 'tale' is a story

☐ 'Tail' and 'tale' are the same

☐ 'Tail' is a fruit, 'tale' is a drink

3.10) How are 'bear' and 'bare' different?

☐ 'Bear' and 'bare' are the same

☐ 'Bear' is an animal, 'bare' means uncovered

☐ 'Bear' is a fruit, 'bare' is a drink

☐ 'Bear' is a color, 'bare' is a food

3.11) What is the difference between 'to' and 'too'?

☐ No difference

☐ 'To' is a preposition, 'too' means also

☐ 'To' and 'too' mean the same

☐ 'To' means also, 'too' is a preposition

3.12) How are 'peace' and 'piece' different?

☐ 'Peace' is calmness, 'piece' is a part of something

☐ 'Peace' is a part of something, 'piece' is calmness

☐ 'Peace' and 'piece' mean the same

☐ No difference

3.13) What does 'right' mean compared to 'write'?

☐ 'Right' is to put down words, 'write' is correct

☐ 'Right' is correct or a direction, 'write' is to put down words

☐ 'Right' and 'write' mean the same

☐ No difference

3.14) Explain the difference between 'week' and 'weak'.

☐ 'Week' is seven days, 'weak' means not strong

☐ No difference

☐ 'Week' and 'weak' mean the same

☐ 'Week' means not strong, 'weak' is seven days

3.15) How do 'rain' and 'reign' differ?

☐ 'Rain' and 'reign' mean the same

☐ 'Rain' is to rule, 'reign' is water from the sky

☐ 'Rain' is water from the sky, 'reign' is to rule

☐ No difference

3.16) What is the difference between 'hole' and 'whole'?

☐ 'Hole' and 'whole' mean the same

☐ No difference

☐ 'Hole' means all of something, 'whole' is an opening

☐ 'Hole' is an opening, 'whole' means all of something

3.17) How are 'meet' and 'meat' different?

☐ 'Meet' is food, 'meat' is to come together

☐ 'Meet' and 'meat' mean the same

☐ 'Meet' is to come together, 'meat' is food

☐ No difference

3.18) What does 'road' mean compared to 'rode'?

☐ 'Road' is past tense of ride, 'rode' is a path for vehicles

☐ 'Road' is a path for vehicles, 'rode' is past tense of ride

☐ No difference

☐ 'Road' and 'rode' mean the same

3.19) Explain the difference between 'sale' and 'sail'.

☐ 'Sale' is selling something, 'sail' is to travel on water

☐ No difference

☐ 'Sale' and 'sail' mean the same

☐ 'Sale' is to travel on water, 'sail' is selling something

3.20) How do 'stare' and 'stair' differ?

☐ No difference

☐ 'Stare' and 'stair' mean the same

☐ 'Stare' is to look hard, 'stair' is a step

☐ 'Stare' is a step, 'stair' is to look hard

3.21) What is the difference between 'new' and 'knew'?

☐ 'New' is past tense of know, 'knew' is recent

☐ 'New' is recent, 'knew' is past tense of know

☐ 'New' and 'knew' mean the same

☐ No difference

3.22) How are 'maid' and 'made' different?

☐ No difference

☐ 'Maid' is a helper, 'made' is past tense of make

☐ 'Maid' is past tense of make, 'made' is a helper

☐ 'Maid' and 'made' mean the same

3.23) What does 'one' mean compared to 'won'?

☐ 'One' is past tense of win, 'won' is a number

☐ 'One' is a number, 'won' is past tense of win

☐ No difference

☐ 'One' and 'won' mean the same

3.24) Explain the difference between 'red' and 'read'.

☐ 'Red' and 'read' mean the same

☐ 'Red' is to look at words, 'read' is a color

☐ No difference

☐ 'Red' is a color, 'read' is to look at words

3.25) How do 'by' and 'buy' differ?

☐ 'By' is to purchase, 'buy' is near

☐ No difference

☐ 'By' is near or next to, 'buy' is to purchase

☐ 'By' and 'buy' mean the same

3.26) What is the difference between 'bye' and 'by'?

☐ No difference

☐ 'Bye' is a farewell, 'by' is near or next to

☐ 'Bye' and 'by' mean the same

☐ 'Bye' is near, 'by' is a farewell

3.27) How are 'cereal' and 'serial' different?

☐ 'Cereal' and 'serial' mean the same

☐ 'Cereal' is a breakfast food, 'serial' is a series

☐ No difference

☐ 'Cereal' is a series, 'serial' is a breakfast food

3.28) What does 'no' mean compared to 'know'?

☐ 'No' and 'know' mean the same

☐ 'No' is to understand, 'know' is a negative response

☐ 'No' is a negative response, 'know' is to understand

☐ No difference

3.29) Explain the difference between 'break' and 'brake'.

☐ No difference

☐ 'Break' is to stop a vehicle, 'brake' is to separate

☐ 'Break' is to separate into pieces, 'brake' is to stop a vehicle

☐ 'Break' and 'brake' mean the same

3.30) How do 'due' and 'dew' differ?

☐ No difference

☐ 'Due' is expected or owed, 'dew' is moisture

☐ 'Due' and 'dew' mean the same

☐ 'Due' is moisture, 'dew' is expected

3.31) What is the difference between 'plain' and 'plane'?

☐ 'Plain' and 'plane' mean the same

☐ 'Plain' is simple or a flat area, 'plane' is an aircraft

☐ No difference

☐ 'Plain' is an aircraft, 'plane' is simple

3.32) How are 'principal' and 'principle' different?

☐ 'Principal' is a rule, 'principle' is a head of school

☐ 'Principal' and 'principle' mean the same

☐ 'Principal' is a head of a school, 'principle' is a rule or belief

☐ No difference

3.33) What does 'sight' mean compared to 'site'?

☐ 'Sight' and 'site' mean the same

☐ 'Sight' is the ability to see, 'site' is a location

☐ 'Sight' is a location, 'site' is the ability to see

☐ No difference

3.34) Explain the difference between 'threw' and 'through'.

☐ 'Threw' is past tense of throw, 'through' means in one side and out the other

☐ 'Threw' and 'through' mean the same

☐ 'Threw' means in one side and out the other, 'through' is past tense of throw

☐ No difference

3.35) How do 'waist' and 'waste' differ?

☐ 'Waist' is a part of the body, 'waste' is to use carelessly

☐ 'Waist' is to use carelessly, 'waste' is a part of the body

☐ No difference

☐ 'Waist' and 'waste' mean the same

3.36) What is the difference between 'beach' and 'beech'?

☐ 'Beach' and 'beech' mean the same

☐ 'Beach' is a sandy shore, 'beech' is a type of tree

☐ 'Beach' is a type of tree, 'beech' is a sandy shore

☐ No difference

3.37) How are 'choir' and 'quire' different?

☐ 'Choir' is a group of singers, 'quire' is a quantity of paper

☐ 'Choir' and 'quire' mean the same

☐ No difference

☐ 'Choir' is a quantity of paper, 'quire' is a group of singers

3.38) What does 'fair' mean compared to 'fare'?

☐ 'Fair' and 'fare' mean the same

☐ No difference

☐ 'Fair' is just or a gathering, 'fare' is a fee or food

☐ 'Fair' is a fee or food, 'fare' is just

3.39) Explain the difference between 'lessen' and 'lesson'.

☐ No difference

☐ 'Lessen' and 'lesson' mean the same

☐ 'Lessen' is to reduce, 'lesson' is something taught

☐ 'Lessen' is something taught, 'lesson' is to reduce

3.40) How do 'sew' and 'sow' differ?

☐ No difference

☐ 'Sew' is to plant seeds, 'sow' is to stitch

☐ 'Sew' is to stitch, 'sow' is to plant seeds

☐ 'Sew' and 'sow' mean the same

Topic 3 - Answers

Question Number	Answer	Explanation
3.1	'Flower' is a plant, 'flour' is ground wheat	'Flower' refers to the colorful part of a plant, while 'flour' is used for baking and cooking.
3.2	'Sea' is a large body of water, 'see' means to look	'Sea' refers to the vast body of saltwater, while 'see' is the act of perceiving visually.
3.3	'Sun' is a star, 'son' is a male child	The 'sun' is the celestial body in the sky, while 'son' refers to a male offspring.
3.4	'Pair' means two of something, 'pear' is a fruit	'Pair' denotes two items together, whereas 'pear' is an edible, sweet fruit.
3.5	'Mail' is letters and packages, 'male' is a gender	'Mail' refers to the postal system, while 'male' denotes a biological sex.
3.6	'Night' is when it's dark, 'knight' is a warrior	'Night' refers to the time of darkness, whereas 'knight' denotes a medieval soldier.
3.7	'Blue' is a color, 'blew' means to blow air	'Blue' is a primary color, while 'blew' is the past tense of blowing air.
3.8	'Hair' is on your head, 'hare' is an animal	'Hair' refers to the strands on heads, while a 'hare' is a mammal similar to a rabbit.
3.9	'Tail' is the end of an animal, 'tale' is a story	'Tail' refers to the rear part of an animal, while 'tale' is a narrative or story.
3.10	'Bear' is an animal, 'bare' means uncovered	A 'bear' is a large mammal, while 'bare' refers to something not covered or naked.
3.11	'To' is a preposition, 'too' means also	'To' indicates direction or place, while 'too' means excessively or also.
3.12	'Peace' is calmness, 'piece' is a part of something	'Peace' refers to tranquility, while a 'piece' is a portion or fragment.
3.13	'Right' is correct or a direction, 'write' is to put down words	'Right' can mean correct or a direction, while 'write' refers to composing text.
3.14	'Week' is seven days, 'weak' means not strong	'Week' refers to a time period, whereas 'weak' denotes lacking strength.
3.15	'Rain' is water from the sky, 'reign' is to rule	'Rain' is precipitation, while 'reign' means to hold royal office or rule.
3.16	'Hole' is an opening, 'whole' means all of something	A 'hole' is a gap or space, while 'whole' refers to complete or entire.
3.17	'Meet' is to come together, 'meat' is food	'Meet' refers to gathering or encountering, whereas 'meat' is animal flesh for food.
3.18	'Road' is a path for vehicles, 'rode' is past tense of ride	A 'road' is a way or route, while 'rode' is the past form of riding.

3.19	'Sale' is selling something, 'sail' is to travel on water	'Sale' refers to the act of selling, while 'sail' means to travel in a boat or ship.
3.20	'Stare' is to look hard, 'stair' is a step	'Stare' means to gaze intently, while a 'stair' is a step or series of steps.
3.21	'New' is recent, 'knew' is past tense of know	'New' refers to something not old or used, while 'knew' is the past of knowing.
3.22	'Maid' is a helper, 'made' is past tense of make	A 'maid' is someone who cleans, while 'made' is the past form of making.
3.23	'One' is a number, 'won' is past tense of win	'One' is the numeral, while 'won' is to have achieved victory.
3.24	'Red' is a color, 'read' is to look at words	'Red' is a primary color, while 'read' is the act of looking at and comprehending text.
3.25	'By' is near or next to, 'buy' is to purchase	'By' indicates proximity, while 'buy' means to acquire by paying.
3.26	'Bye' is a farewell, 'by' is near or next to	'Bye' is used to express goodbye, while 'by' denotes proximity or through.
3.27	'Cereal' is a breakfast food, 'serial' is a series	'Cereal' is eaten at breakfast, while 'serial' refers to something in a series.
3.28	'No' is a negative response, 'know' is to understand	'No' is used to negate, while 'know' means to be aware or understand.
3.29	'Break' is to separate into pieces, 'brake' is to stop a vehicle	'Break' means to divide, while 'brake' is to slow or stop a vehicle.
3.30	'Due' is expected or owed, 'dew' is moisture	'Due' means owed or scheduled, while 'dew' is water droplets formed at night.
3.31	'Plain' is simple or a flat area, 'plane' is an aircraft	'Plain' can be simple or an area, while 'plane' is a vehicle that flies.
3.32	'Principal' is a head of a school, 'principle' is a rule or belief	'Principal' is a school leader, while 'principle' is a fundamental truth or rule.
3.33	'Sight' is the ability to see, 'site' is a location	'Sight' is visual perception, while 'site' refers to a specific place.
3.34	'Threw' is past tense of throw, 'through' means in one side and out the other	'Threw' is to have propelled, while 'through' indicates moving in and out or by means of.
3.35	'Waist' is a part of the body, 'waste' is to use carelessly	The 'waist' is a body part, while 'waste' is to use something without care.
3.36	'Beach' is a sandy shore, 'beech' is a type of tree	A 'beach' is the sandy area by water, while 'beech' is a kind of tree.
3.37	'Choir' is a group of singers, 'quire' is a quantity of paper	A 'choir' is a singing group, while a 'quire' refers to a set of sheets of paper.
3.38	'Fair' is just or a gathering, 'fare' is a fee or food	'Fair' can mean equitable or an event, while 'fare' is cost or type of food.
3.39	'Lessen' is to reduce, 'lesson' is something taught	To 'lessen' is to make smaller, while a 'lesson' is a teaching segment or instruction.
3.40	'Sew' is to stitch, 'sow' is to plant seeds	'Sew' is to join with thread, while 'sow' is to scatter seeds for growing.

Topic 4 – Story Elements

4.1) What is a character in a story?

☐ The place where the story happens

☐ The problem in the story

☐ A person or animal in the story

☐ A funny joke

4.2) What does 'setting' mean in a story?

☐ A scary moment

☐ The end of the story

☐ Where and when the story takes place

☐ The main person in the story

4.3) What is a plot in a story?

☐ A picture in the book

☐ The events in the story

☐ The place where the story happens

☐ A person in the story

4.4) How can you describe a main character?

☐ A small part of the story

☐ The last part of the story

☐ A color

☐ The most important person or animal

4.5) What is the importance of a story's setting?

☐ It ends the story

☐ It names the characters

☐ It sets the time and place

☐ It tells the jokes

4.6) How does a plot develop in a story?

☐ Only the happy parts

☐ Only the sad parts

☐ Beginning, middle, end with events

☐ Pictures only

4.7) What might a character in a story do?

☐ Stay still

☐ Tell jokes only

☐ Talk, move, have adventures

☐ Disappear

4.8) Why is the setting important to a story?

☐ It adds color

☐ It makes the story funny

☐ It's not important

☐ It shows where the events happen

4.9) What could be a problem in a story's plot?

☐ A picture in the book

☐ A challenge or conflict

☐ A funny joke

☐ The title of the story

4.10) How do characters affect the plot of a story?

☐ They write the book

☐ They only watch

☐ They make the events happen

☐ They draw the pictures

4.11) What can a setting tell you about a story?

☐ Time and place of the events

☐ The color of the cover

☐ The title of the story

☐ The last page of the book

4.12) How can you tell who the main character is in a story?

☐ They are the funniest

☐ They are in most of the story

☐ They are only on the first page

☐ They are the tallest

4.13) What is the climax of a story?

☐ The index of the book

☐ The most exciting or important part

☐ The setting

☐ The beginning

4.14) Can a story have more than one setting?

☐ Only if it's a mystery

☐ Yes, it can change

☐ Only in long books

☐ No, only one setting

4.15) How does a character change throughout a story?

☐ They disappear

☐ They grow, learn, or change

☐ They stay the same

☐ They become the setting

4.16) What is a conflict in a story?

☐ The title

☐ A joke

☐ A problem or challenge

☐ The list of chapters

4.17) How does the setting influence the plot?

☐ It influences the events and actions

☐ No influence

☐ It makes the book thicker

☐ It adds pictures

4.18) What role do supporting characters play in a story?

☐ They help the main character

☐ They draw the pictures

☐ They are not important

☐ They read the book

4.19) Can the setting of a story be in the future?

☐ Yes, it can be anywhere

☐ Only in non-fiction

☐ No, only in the past

☐ Only if it's funny

4.20) What is the resolution in a story?

☐ The beginning

☐ The end or solution to the problem

☐ The longest chapter

☐ The table of contents

4.21) What is a 'narrator' in a story?

☐ The person who tells the story

☐ A type of character

☐ A part of the setting

☐ The main character

4.22) How do illustrations help tell a story?

☐ To make the book longer

☐ Only to color the book

☐ They don't help

☐ Show what characters and places look like

4.23) Can a story have more than one problem?

☐ Only if it's a mystery

☐ Yes, it can have many problems

☐ Only in long books

☐ No, only one problem

4.24) How is the beginning of a story important?

☐ It has all the jokes

☐ It's the shortest part

☐ Introduces characters and setting

☐ It's not important

4.25) What does the ending of a story usually do?

☐ Is the longest part

☐ Starts a new story

☐ Solves the problem or finishes the story

☐ Introduces new characters

4.26) Can the setting of a story be a different planet?

☐ No, only on Earth

☐ Only in non-fiction books

☐ Only if it's funny

☐ Yes, it can be anywhere

4.27) What makes a character 'dynamic'?

☐ They disappear

☐ They stay the same

☐ They become less important

☐ They change or grow during the story

4.28) How can dialogue between characters develop the story?

☐ It's not important

☐ Shows characters' thoughts and feelings

☐ It's only in comic books

☐ It's only for jokes

4.29) What is a 'theme' in a story?

☐ The title of the book

☐ A character in the story

☐ The main idea or message

☐ The setting of the story

4.30) How can the weather be part of a story's setting?

☐ Only if it's raining

☐ Shows the time and mood of the story

☐ It doesn't matter

☐ Only in weather books

4.31) How does a character's personality affect a story?

☐ Only affects the end

☐ It shapes their actions and the story's events

☐ Makes the story funny

☐ No effect

4.32) What can a story's title tell you?

☐ Nothing

☐ The number of pages

☐ Hints about the story's content or theme

☐ Only the main character's name

4.33) Can animals be characters in a story?

☐ No, never

☐ Only in non-fiction

☐ Yes, they can be main or supporting characters

☐ Only in picture books

4.34) What is the purpose of a plot twist?

☐ No purpose

☐ To add surprise or change the story's direction

☐ To introduce new characters

☐ To end the story

4.35) How can the time of day be part of a story's setting?

☐ Tells the time

☐ Shows the weather

☐ Sets the scene and mood

☐ No importance

4.36) What role do villains play in a story?

☐ Only to scare

☐ To draw pictures

☐ Create conflict or challenges for the hero

☐ To make the story funny

4.37) Can a story be told without words?

☐ Only for young children

☐ Yes, through pictures or silent films

☐ Only in comic books

☐ No, words are necessary

4.38) How does the author's style influence a story?

☐ It adds a unique voice or tone to the story

☐ Only changes the title

☐ No influence

☐ Makes the story longer

4.39) What is the role of a sidekick in a story?

☐ Draws the pictures

☐ Is the main villain

☐ No role

☐ Helps or supports the main character

4.40) Can the mood of a story change?

☐ No, always the same

☐ Only at the end

☐ Only if it's funny

☐ Yes, it can change throughout the story

Topic 4 - Answers

Question Number	Answer	Explanation
4.1	A person or animal in the story	Characters are the individuals in a story, including people and animals, who carry out the actions.
4.2	Where and when the story takes place	The setting provides the backdrop of the story, including its time period and location.
4.3	The events in the story	The plot is the sequence of events and actions that make up the story.
4.4	The most important person or animal	The main character is central to the story and often drives the narrative forward.
4.5	It sets the time and place	The setting establishes the context for the story, impacting the events and character interactions.
4.6	Beginning, middle, end with events	The plot develops through a structured sequence, typically including a beginning, middle, and end.
4.7	Talk, move, have adventures	Characters engage in various activities and decisions that drive the story.
4.8	It shows where the events happen	The setting influences the plot and can affect the characters' behaviors and the story's direction.
4.9	A challenge or conflict	Problems in the plot are obstacles or challenges that characters need to resolve or overcome.
4.10	They make the events happen	Characters are essential for progressing the plot through their actions and decisions.
4.11	Time and place of the events	The setting indicates when and where the story's events take place, adding context.
4.12	They are in most of the story	The main character typically appears throughout the story and is central to the plot.
4.13	The most exciting or important part	The climax is the peak of the story where the main conflict reaches its highest tension.
4.14	Yes, it can change	A story can have multiple settings, changing as the plot progresses to different locations or times.
4.15	They grow, learn, or change	Characters often develop or transform throughout the story, experiencing personal growth or change.
4.16	A problem or challenge	Conflict in a story is the struggle or challenge faced by the characters, driving the narrative.
4.17	It influences the events and actions	The setting can shape the story's events and affect how characters act and react.
4.18	They help the main character	Supporting characters contribute to the story by assisting or interacting with the main character.

4.19	Yes, it can be anywhere	The setting of a story can be imaginative, including futuristic or fantastical locations.
4.20	The end or solution to the problem	The resolution concludes the story, resolving conflicts and tying up loose ends.
4.21	The person who tells the story	The narrator is the voice that conveys the story to the reader, providing perspective.
4.22	Show what characters and places look like	Illustrations enhance storytelling by visually depicting characters, settings, and events.
4.23	Yes, it can have many problems	A story can involve multiple conflicts or challenges, adding complexity to the plot.
4.24	Introduces characters and setting	The beginning of a story sets the stage, introducing key characters and the setting.
4.25	Solves the problem or finishes the story	The ending typically resolves the story's conflicts and provides closure to the narrative.
4.26	Yes, it can be anywhere	Story settings can be diverse and imaginative, including other planets or fictional worlds.
4.27	They change or grow during the story	Dynamic characters undergo significant personal growth or changes throughout the story.
4.28	Shows characters' thoughts and feelings	Dialogue reveals characters' perspectives and emotions, contributing to character development and the plot.
4.29	The main idea or message	The theme is the central message or underlying idea of the story, often conveying morals or insights.
4.30	Shows the time and mood of the story	The weather in a story's setting can set the mood and contribute to the atmosphere.
4.31	It shapes their actions and the story's events	A character's personality influences their decisions and interactions, impacting the plot.
4.32	Hints about the story's content or theme	The title often provides clues about the story's subject matter or themes.
4.33	Yes, they can be main or supporting characters	Animals can serve as characters in stories, often with human-like qualities or roles.
4.34	To add surprise or change the story's direction	A plot twist introduces unexpected changes that alter the course of the story.
4.35	Sets the scene and mood	The time of day in a story's setting can influence the atmosphere and mood of the narrative.
4.36	Create conflict or challenges for the hero	Villains often serve as antagonists, presenting obstacles or conflicts for the protagonist.
4.37	Yes, through pictures or silent films	Stories can be conveyed without words, using visual storytelling like pictures or mime.
4.38	It adds a unique voice or tone to the story	The author's style gives a distinctive quality to the story, affecting how it is perceived and enjoyed.
4.39	Helps or supports the main character	Sidekicks provide support to main characters, often aiding them in their journey or challenges.
4.40	Yes, it can change throughout the story	The mood of a story can vary, shifting in tone and atmosphere as the plot progresses.

Topic 5 – Points of View

5.1) Who is usually the narrator in a first-person story?

☐ A character in the story

☐ The author

☐ An outside observer

☐ The main character's friend

5.2) What does "first-person" mean in a story?

☐ The story is about the first person

☐ The story is told by an observer

☐ The story is told by a character in it

☐ The story is set in the past

5.3) How can you tell a story is written in third-person?

☐ It uses "he", "she", or "they"

☐ It uses "I" or "me"

☐ It is told by the main character

☐ It is about a third person

5.4) Why might an author choose to write in first-person?

☐ To show all characters' thoughts

☐ To make the story more exciting

☐ To give a personal view of the story

☐ To tell the story faster

5.5) What is a third-person narrative?

☐ A story told by the main character

☐ A story about three people

☐ A story told by someone not in the story

☐ A story told in the past

5.6) Can a story have both first-person and third-person parts?

☐ No, it's not possible

☐ Yes, but only in novels

☐ Yes, if the author chooses to

☐ No, because it confuses readers

5.7) In first-person narrative, who is telling the story?

☐ The author

☐ The main character

☐ An observer

☐ A narrator

5.8) Why do some stories use third-person?

☐ To limit the viewpoint

☐ To tell the story quickly

☐ To show different perspectives

☐ To focus on one character

5.9) What point of view is used when "I" and "me" are in the story?

☐ Second-person

☐ Third-person

☐ First-person

☐ Fourth-person

5.10) How does first-person point of view affect a story?

☐ It shows only one character's thoughts

☐ It tells the story faster

☐ It makes the story less interesting

☐ It includes many different perspectives

5.11) What point of view tells the story from the perspective of 'you'?

☐ First-person

☐ Second-person

☐ Third-person

☐ Fourth-person

5.12) When a story is told in third-person, what can the narrator do?

☐ Talk about their feelings

☐ Show thoughts of all characters

☐ Use 'I' and 'me'

☐ Speak directly to the reader

5.13) In which point of view is the narrator a part of the story?

☐ First-person

☐ Second-person

☐ Third-person

☐ None of these

5.14) Which point of view is less common in stories?

☐ First-person

☐ Second-person

☐ Third-person

☐ All are equally common

5.15) How does third-person limited differ from third-person omniscient?

☐ Narrator knows everything

☐ Narrator tells the story faster

☐ Narrator only knows one character's thoughts

☐ Narrator is a character in the story

5.16) Why would an author choose second-person point of view?

☐ To make the reader feel part of the story

☐ To show different characters' thoughts

☐ To tell the story more quickly

☐ To describe the main character

5.17) What is a sign that a story is in first-person?

☐ It uses 'he' or 'she'

☐ It talks about the author

☐ It uses 'I' or 'me'

☐ It is about a narrator

5.18) How can you tell who is telling the story?

☐ It always tells you at the start

☐ Inferring from pronouns

☐ The author is always telling the story

☐ It will change form page to page all the time

5.19) What does third-person omniscient mean?

☐ Narrator is all-knowing

☐ Narrator is in the story

☐ Narrator talks to the reader

☐ Narrator only knows one character

5.20) How does second-person point of view affect a story?

☐ Makes it more interactive

☐ Focuses on one character

☐ Shows many perspectives

☐ Tells the story faster

5.21) What is the main feature of first-person narrative?

☐ Narrator is not in the story

☐ Narrator knows everything

☐ Narrator is a character in the story

☐ Narrator does not like the main character

5.22) Which narrative point of view can make the reader feel like an observer?

☐ First-person

☐ Second-person

☐ Third-person

☐ Fourth-person

5.23) What does third-person limited point of view mean?

☐ Narrator knows limited information

☐ Narrator is limited to one place

☐ Narrator only speaks to one character

☐ Narrator tells a limited story

5.24) Can a narrator be unreliable in first-person narrative?

☐ Yes, but only if they tell you

☐ No, because they are always honest

☐ Yes, if they are not telling the truth

☐ No, because they are the main character

5.25) Why might a story be told in second-person?

☐ To give instructions

☐ To describe the narrator

☐ To make the story longer

☐ To focus on the main character

5.26) What does it mean when a story is told in third-person omniscient?

☐ The narrator knows some things

☐ The narrator is guessing

☐ The narrator knows everything

☐ The narrator is part of the story

5.27) Which narrative perspective is used the most in novels?

☐ First-person

☐ Second-person

☐ Third-person

☐ All are used equally

5.28) What is the effect of a first-person narrative on the story?

☐ Makes it less believable

☐ Gives insight into one character

☐ Shows all characters' thoughts

☐ Makes the story very short

5.29) Can a story in first-person show other characters' thoughts?

☐ Yes, always

☐ No, only the narrator's thoughts

☐ Yes, if the narrator guesses

☐ No, unless the narrator is told

5.30) Why is third-person used in many children's books?

☐ To teach about the third person

☐ To make the story simpler

☐ To offer different viewpoints

☐ To focus on the main character

5.31) In first-person narrative, what pronouns are typically used?

☐ He, She

☐ You, Your

☐ I, Me

☐ They, Them

5.32) What is a benefit of using third-person omniscient?

☐ Narrator can only see one perspective

☐ Narrator knows the thoughts of all characters

☐ Narrator is part of the story

☐ Narrator speaks directly to the reader

5.33) Can a story switch from first-person to third-person?

☐ No, it's confusing

☐ Yes, to show different perspectives

☐ No, it's against the rules

☐ Yes, but only in movies

5.34) What effect does second-person point of view have on a reader?

☐ Makes them feel detached

☐ Puts them in the story

☐ Tells them about the author

☐ Shows them all characters' thoughts

5.35) Why might an author switch points of view in a story?

☐ To confuse the reader

☐ To show different characters' perspectives

☐ Because they forgot the original point of view

☐ To make the story shorter

5.36) How does first-person point of view limit a story?

☐ It can't show other characters' thoughts

☐ It makes the story too long

☐ It only talks about the past

☐ It doesn't show any emotions

5.37) What point of view is common in autobiographies?

☐ First-person

☐ Second-person

☐ Third-person

☐ Fourth-person

5.38) How can third-person limited affect a story?

☐ By knowing everything

☐ By focusing on one character

☐ By telling the story faster

☐ By using 'I' and 'me'

5.39) What is the narrator's role in a second-person narrative?

☐ To describe themselves

☐ To talk about the author

☐ To address the reader as 'you'

☐ To tell their own story

5.40) What does first-person point of view add to a memoir?

☐ Unreliability

☐ Multiple perspectives

☐ Personal experience

☐ Quick storytelling

Topic 5 - Answers

Question Number	Answer	Explanation
5.1	A character in the story	In first-person, the story is typically narrated by a character.
5.2	The story is told by a character in it	First-person means the narrator is a part of the story's world.
5.3	It uses "he", "she", or "they"	Third-person narratives use third-person pronouns.
5.4	To give a personal view of the story	First-person can provide a closer, more personal perspective.
5.5	A story told by someone not in the story	In third-person, the narrator is not part of the story's events.
5.6	Yes, if the author chooses to	Authors can mix narrative styles for creative purposes.
5.7	The main character	In first-person, the story is typically told by the protagonist.
5.8	To show different perspectives	Third-person allows for a broader view of the story's world.
5.9	First-person	"I" and "me" are indicative of a first-person perspective.
5.10	It shows only one character's thoughts	First-person is limited to the narrator's perspective.
5.11	Second-person	"You" is used in second-person narratives.
5.12	Show thoughts of all characters	Third-person can provide insights into multiple characters.
5.13	First-person	The narrator is part of the story in a first-person narrative.
5.14	Second-person	Second-person is less commonly used in storytelling.
5.15	Narrator only knows one character's thoughts	Third-person limited is restricted to one viewpoint.
5.16	To make the reader feel part of the story	Second-person can engage the reader directly.
5.17	It uses 'I' or 'me'	These pronouns signify a first-person narrative.
5.18	Inferring from pronouns	Normally we use pronouns to tell who is telling the story, such as I, he, or they.

5.19	Narrator is all-knowing	Omniscient narrators have a god-like knowledge of the story.
5.20	Makes it more interactive	Second-person involves the reader in the story's action.
5.21	Narrator is a character in the story	First-person narratives are told from a character's viewpoint.
5.22	Third-person	Third-person can make the reader feel like an onlooker.
5.23	Narrator knows limited information	Limited point of view restricts the narrative to certain knowledge.
5.24	Yes, if they are not telling the truth	First-person narrators can be biased or unreliable.
5.25	To give instructions	Second-person can direct the reader's actions or thoughts.
5.26	The narrator knows everything	Omniscient narrators have complete knowledge of the story's events.
5.27	Third-person	Third-person is a commonly used perspective in novels.
5.28	Gives insight into one character	First-person allows deep exploration of one character's experience.
5.29	No, only the narrator's thoughts	First-person is limited to the narrator's perspective and knowledge.
5.30	To offer different viewpoints	Third-person can provide a broader view suitable for children's books.
5.31	I, Me	These pronouns are typical of a first-person narrative.
5.32	Narrator knows the thoughts of all characters	Omniscient viewpoint offers insight into every character's mind.
5.33	Yes, to show different perspectives	Changing points of view can provide various angles of the story.
5.34	Puts them in the story	Second-person narratives directly involve the reader in the events.
5.35	To show different characters' perspectives	Varying points of view can enhance the story's depth and dimension
5.36	It can't show other characters' thoughts	First-person is confined to the narrator's experiences and thoughts.
5.37	First-person	Autobiographies are often written from the author's perspective.
5.38	By focusing on one character	Third-person limited delves deeply into one character's inner world.
5.39	To address the reader as 'you'	In second-person, the narrator speaks directly to the reader.
5.40	Personal experience	First-person adds authenticity and intimacy to memoirs.

Topic 6 - Summarizing Texts

In a small village, there was a curious cat named Whiskers. Whiskers loved to explore the village and meet new friends. One day, Whiskers stumbled upon a mysterious house at the edge of the village. The house was old and seemed abandoned. Inside, Whiskers found a strange box that glowed with a soft light. When he touched the box, it opened to reveal a magical key. He was so elated to find such a magical object. Whiskers took the key and suddenly, the house was filled with colorful lights and sounds. The key turned out to be magical and it gave Whiskers the ability to understand and talk to humans.

6.1) What did Whiskers discover in the mysterious house?

☐ A magical key

☐ A hidden treasure

☐ A lost cat

☐ A flower

6.2) Where did the story take place?

☐ In a small village

☐ In a big city

☐ In a forest

☐ On a farm

6.3) What was special about the item?

☐ It was very old

☐ It glowed in the dark

☐ It could talk

☐ It gave Whiskers magical abilities

6.4) How did Whiskers feel when he found the item?

☐ Scared

☐ Excited

☐ Sad

☐ Angry

6.5) What happened to the house when Whiskers found the key?

☐ It disappeared

☐ It turned colorful

☐ It became a castle

☐ Nothing happened

Tommy was a young boy who loved adventure. He lived near a forest where he often played and explored. One sunny afternoon, while looking around for a something exciting, Tommy found a hidden path in the forest that he had never seen before. Following the path, he discovered a clearing with a beautiful pond. In the pond, he saw fish of all colors and sizes swimming happily. Tommy sat by the pond for hours, watching the fish and listening to the sounds of nature. He felt a deep connection with the forest and its creatures. From that day on, Tommy decided to become a protector of the forest, taking care of its animals and plants.

6.6) What did Tommy find in the forest?

☐ A hidden path and a pond

☐ A treasure map

☐ A lost puppy

☐ A magical tree

6.7) How did Tommy feel in the forest?

☐ Afraid

☐ Curious

☐ Bored

☐ Happy

6.8) What was special about the pond?

☐ It had a waterfall

☐ It was very deep

☐ It had colorful fish

☐ It was dry

6.9) What decision did Tommy make after visiting the pond?

☐ To become a forest protector

☐ To visit the pond every day

☐ To tell his friends about it

☐ To build a house there

6.10) What is the main theme of the story?

☐ Friendship

☐ Fun

☐ Magic

☐ Protection of nature

Amy loved to bake with her grandmother. Every Saturday, they would try a new recipe. This week, they decided to bake chocolate chip cookies. They mixed the dough, added chocolate chips, and shaped the cookies. While the cookies were baking, Amy and her grandmother cleaned up the kitchen. The smell of baking cookies filled the house, making everyone excited. When the cookies were done, they were crispy on the outside and chewy on the inside. Amy's family loved the cookies, and it was a perfect end to a fun baking day.

6.11) What did Amy and her grandmother bake?

☐ Pancakes

☐ Chocolate chip cookies

☐ A cake

☐ Bread

6.12) How often did Amy bake with her grandmother?

☐ Every day

☐ Every Saturday

☐ Once a month

☐ On holidays

6.13) What was special about the cookies?

☐ They were very large

☐ They were crispy and chewy

☐ They had no sugar

☐ They were shaped like animals

6.14) What did Amy and her grandmother do while the cookies baked?

☐ Watched TV

☐ Went to the store

☐ Cleaned the kitchen

☐ Played a game

6.15) How did Amy's family feel about the cookies?

☐ They didn't like them

☐ They thought they were okay

☐ They loved them

☐ They were too sweet

In a small town, there was a library loved by all. The librarian, Mr. Brown, was kind and helpful. Every Friday, Mr. Brown organized a story hour for children. Children would gather around as Mr. Brown read stories full of adventure and magic. One day, he read a story about a pirate treasure. The children were so inspired that they decided to have a treasure hunt in the library. With Mr. Brown's help, they set up clues and riddles around the library. The treasure hunt was a huge success, and the children found the 'treasure' - a box of new books to read.

6.16) Who was Mr. Brown?

☐ A teacher

☐ A librarian

☐ A baker

☐ A doctor

6.17) What special event did Mr. Brown organize?

☐ A reading contest

☐ A story hour

☐ A music festival

☐ A sports day

6.18) What inspired the children's treasure hunt?

☐ A movie

☐ A story about pirates

☐ A game

☐ A history book

6.19) Where did the treasure hunt take place?

☐ In a park

☐ In the library

☐ In a school

☐ In a garden

6.20) What was the 'treasure' the children found?

☐ Gold coins

☐ Candy

☐ New books

☐ Toys

Lily and Max were best friends who loved exploring nature. One summer day, they decided to hike up a nearby hill. As they climbed, they noticed different types of flowers and birds. At the top of the hill, they found a small pond with clear water. Near the pond, there was a bench where they sat and ate their lunch. They talked about their adventure and how much they enjoyed the hike. On their way down, they picked up litter to keep the hill clean. Lily and Max promised to come back again and continue exploring the beauty of nature.

6.21) What did Lily and Max do one summer day?

☐ Went swimming

☐ Visited a zoo

☐ Hiked up a hill

☐ Played in the park

6.22) What did they find at the top of the hill?

☐ A playground

☐ A small pond

☐ A treehouse

☐ A cave

6.23) What did they do to help the environment?

☐ Planted a tree

☐ Built a birdhouse

☐ Picked up litter

☐ Watered plants

6.24) How did Lily and Max feel about their hike?

☐ They were bored

☐ They were excited

☐ They were scared

☐ They were happy

6.25) What did they plan to do in the future?

☐ Never hike again

☐ Come back for more exploration

☐ Write a story about it

☐ Draw a map of the hill

Ben was a young artist who loved painting. His favorite subject was the ocean. He would sit by the seaside and paint the waves, the sky, and the boats. One day, he decided to enter his best painting in a local art competition. Ben worked hard, adding details to make the painting perfect. On the day of the competition, he was nervous but excited. Many people admired Ben's painting, and it won first prize. Winning the competition inspired Ben to keep painting and sharing his love for the ocean.

6.26) What was Ben's favorite subject to paint?

☐ Forests

☐ Mountains

☐ The ocean

☐ Cities

6.27) Where did Ben like to paint?

☐ In his studio

☐ By the seaside

☐ In a park

☐ At school

6.28) What did Ben do for the art competition?

☐ Took a photograph

☐ Made a sculpture

☐ Entered a painting

☐ Wrote a poem

6.29) How did Ben feel on the day of the competition?

☐ Confused

☐ Angry

☐ Nervous but excited

☐ Sad

6.30) What was the outcome of the competition for Ben?

☐ He lost

☐ He won first prize

☐ He forgot his painting

☐ He was disqualified

Max was a young inventor who lived in a coastal town. He loved to create gadgets and machines. His latest invention was a robot that could clean beaches. Max named the robot Sandy. Together, Max and Sandy cleaned the beaches every morning, picking up trash and helping sea animals. One day, they found a sea turtle tangled in fishing nets. With Sandy's help, Max freed the turtle. The turtle was grateful and swam away happily. This experience made Max even more determined to help the environment. He decided to build more robots like Sandy to clean beaches all over the world. Max's inventions made a big difference in protecting marine life and keeping the beaches clean.

6.31) What was Max's latest invention?

☐ A flying car

☐ A beach-cleaning robot

☐ A talking dog

☐ A magic wand

6.32) What did Max and his robot do together?

☐ Went fishing

☐ Cleaned beaches

☐ Built sandcastles

☐ Played volleyball

6.33) What did they find on the beach one day?

☐ A treasure chest

☐ A lost child

☐ A sea turtle in a net

☐ A message in a bottle

6.34) How did Max and Sandy help the sea turtle?

☐ Gave it food

☐ Took it home

☐ Freed it from the nets

☐ Taught it to swim

6.35) What impact did Max's invention have?

☐ It scared the sea animals

☐ It made the beach dirty

☐ It helped protect marine life

☐ It caused noise pollution

6.36) What did Max decide to do after helping the turtle?

☐ Go on vacation

☐ Stop inventing

☐ Build more robots like Sandy

☐ Write a book

6.37) What is the main theme of the story?

☐ Adventure at sea

☐ The importance of recycling

☐ Protecting the environment

☐ The fun of building robots

6.38) How did the turtle feel after being freed?

☐ Angry

☐ Scared

☐ Grateful

☐ Sad

6.39) What kind of person is Max?

☐ Lazy

☐ Curious and helpful

☐ Scared of animals

☐ Forgetful

6.40) What did Max's inventions do for the beaches?

☐ Made them popular

☐ Turned them into parks

☐ Kept them clean

☐ Closed them to the public

Topic 6 - Answers

Question Number	Answer	Explanation
6.1	A magical key	Whiskers found a key that gave him magical abilities.
6.2	In a small village	The story is set in a small village.
6.3	It gave Whiskers magical abilities	The key allowed Whiskers to understand and talk to humans.
6.4	Excited	Whiskers was likely excited to find something magical.
6.5	It turned colorful	The house filled with colorful lights and sounds.
6.6	A hidden path and a pond	Tommy found a hidden path leading to a pond.
6.7	Curious	Tommy was looking for a new adventure in the forest, meaning he was curious
6.8	It had colorful fish	The pond had fish of all colors and sizes.
6.9	To become a forest protector	Tommy decided to protect the forest and its inhabitants.
6.10	Protection of nature	The story's main theme is about protecting nature.
6.11	Chocolate chip cookies	They baked chocolate chip cookies.
6.12	Every Saturday	Amy and her grandmother baked together every Saturday.
6.13	They were crispy and chewy	The cookies were crispy outside and chewy inside.
6.14	Cleaned the kitchen	They cleaned up while the cookies were baking.
6.15	They loved them	Amy's family enjoyed the cookies.
6.16	A librarian	Mr. Brown was a librarian.
6.17	A story hour	He organized a story hour for children.
6.18	A story about pirates	A pirate treasure story inspired the treasure hunt.

6.19	In the library	The treasure hunt was set up in the library.
6.20	New books	The 'treasure' was a box of new books.
6.21	Hiked up a hill	Lily and Max decided to hike up a hill.
6.22	A small pond	They found a small pond at the top of the hill.
6.23	Picked up litter	They collected litter to keep the hill clean.
6.24	They were happy	They enjoyed the hike and felt happy.
6.25	Come back for more exploration	They planned to return and continue exploring.
6.26	The ocean	Ben loved painting the ocean.
6.27	By the seaside	He painted by the seaside.
6.28	Entered a painting	He entered his best painting in the competition.
6.29	Nervous but excited	He felt a mix of nerves and excitement.
6.30	He won first prize	His painting won the first prize.
6.31	A beach-cleaning robot	Max invented a robot to clean beaches.
6.32	Cleaned beaches	Max and Sandy cleaned the beaches together.
6.33	A sea turtle in a net	They found a sea turtle tangled in fishing nets.
6.34	Freed it from the nets	They helped the turtle by freeing it.
6.35	It helped protect marine life	Max's invention contributed to protecting marine life.
6.36	Build more robots like Sandy	He decided to create more cleaning robots.
6.37	Protecting the environment	The main theme is environmental protection.
6.38	Grateful	The turtle was grateful after being freed.
6.39	Curious and helpful	Max is portrayed as curious and eager to help.
6.40	Kept them clean	The robots helped in keeping the beaches clean.

Topic 7 – Synonyms and Antonyms

7.1) What is a synonym for 'happy'?

☐ Sad

☐ Angry

☐ Joyful

☐ Tired

7.2) What is the antonym of 'big'?

☐ Small

☐ Huge

☐ Giant

☐ Massive

7.3) Find a synonym for 'fast'.

☐ Slow

☐ Quick

☐ Heavy

☐ Weak

7.4) What is the antonym of 'hard'?

☐ Soft

☐ Difficult

☐ Tough

☐ Strong

7.5) Choose a synonym for 'funny'.

☐ Boring

☐ Serious

☐ Hilarious

☐ Sad

7.6) What is the antonym of 'old'?

☐ New

☐ Ancient

☐ Young

☐ Historical

7.7) Find a synonym for 'cold'.

☐ Hot

☐ Chilly

☐ Warm

☐ Boiling

7.8) What is the antonym of 'thin'?

☐ Slim

☐ Thick

☐ Narrow

☐ Skinny

7.9) Choose a synonym for 'smart'.

☐ Dumb

☐ Intelligent

☐ Silly

☐ Clumsy

7.10) What is the antonym of 'light'?

☐ Bright

☐ Heavy

☐ Shiny

☐ Glowing

7.11) What is a synonym for 'strong'?

☐ Weak

☐ Powerful

☐ Lazy

☐ Quiet

7.12) What is the antonym of 'wet'?

☐ Dry

☐ Damp

☐ Soaked

☐ Moist

7.13) Find a synonym for 'tiny'.

☐ Small

☐ Huge

☐ Gigantic

☐ Large

7.14) What is the antonym of 'full'?

☐ Empty

☐ Overflowing

☐ Packed

☐ Bursting

7.15) Choose a synonym for 'easy'.

☐ Simple

☐ Hard

☐ Difficult

☐ Complex

7.16) What is the antonym of 'young'?

☐ Old

☐ New

☐ Fresh

☐ Modern

7.17) Find a synonym for 'clean'.

☐ Dirty

☐ Spotless

☐ Messy

☐ Cluttered

7.18) What is the antonym of 'bright'?

☐ Dull

☐ Shiny

☐ Glowing

☐ Luminous

7.19) Choose a synonym for 'quiet'.

☐ Noisy

☐ Loud

☐ Silent

☐ Raucous

7.20) What is the antonym of 'begin'?

☐ Start

☐ End

☐ Continue

☐ Initiate

7.21) What is a synonym for 'excited'?

☐ Bored

☐ Thrilled

☐ Uninterested

☐ Indifferent

7.22) What is the antonym of 'smooth'?

☐ Rough

☐ Soft

☐ Silky

☐ Glossy

7.23) Find a synonym for 'large'.

☐ Huge

☐ Tiny

☐ Small

☐ Narrow

7.24) What is the antonym of 'rich'?

☐ Wealthy

☐ Poor

☐ Prosperous

☐ Affluent

7.25) Choose a synonym for 'difficult'.

☐ Easy

☐ Hard

☐ Simple

☐ Effortless

7.26) What is the antonym of 'hot'?

☐ Warm

☐ Cold

☐ Boiling

☐ Scorching

7.27) Find a synonym for 'fun'.

☐ Boring

☐ Enjoyable

☐ Tedious

☐ Dreary

7.28) What is the antonym of 'friendly'?

☐ Kind

☐ Hostile

☐ Nice

☐ Amicable

7.29) Choose a synonym for 'scary'.

☐ Terrifying

☐ Comforting

☐ Pleasant

☐ Calm

7.30) What is the antonym of 'sharp'?

☐ Dull

☐ Pointed

☐ Cutting

☐ Edgy

7.31) What is a synonym for 'angry'?

☐ Furious

☐ Happy

☐ Pleased

☐ Joyful

7.32) What is the antonym of 'deep'?

☐ Shallow

☐ Wide

☐ Narrow

☐ Broad

7.33) Find a synonym for 'clever'.

☐ Stupid

☐ Intelligent

☐ Silly

☐ Dull

7.34) What is the antonym of 'near'?

☐ Close

☐ Far

☐ Next

☐ Adjacent

7.35) Choose a synonym for 'tasty'.

☐ Delicious

☐ Bland

☐ Unpleasant

☐ Bitter

7.36) What is the antonym of 'safe'?

☐ Secure

☐ Dangerous

☐ Protected

☐ Guarded

7.37) Find a synonym for 'sad'.

☐ Happy

☐ Joyful

☐ Miserable

☐ Cheerful

7.38) What is the antonym of 'open'?

☐ Top

☐ Shut

☐ Locked

☐ Sealed

7.39) Choose a synonym for 'lazy'.

☐ Active

☐ Slothful

☐ Energetic

☐ Industrious

7.40) What is the antonym of 'high'?

☐ Low

☐ Tall

☐ Elevated

☐ Soaring

Topic 7 – Answers

Question Number	Answer	Explanation
7.1	Joyful	'Joyful' means feeling, expressing, or causing great pleasure and happiness, similar to 'happy'.
7.2	Small	'Small' is the opposite of 'big'.
7.3	Quick	'Quick' is another word for 'fast'.
7.4	Soft	'Soft' is the opposite of 'hard'.
7.5	Hilarious	'Hilarious' means extremely funny, just like 'funny'.
7.6	New	'New' is the opposite of 'old'.
7.7	Chilly	'Chilly' is another word for 'cold'.
7.8	Thick	'Thick' is the opposite of 'thin'.
7.9	Intelligent	'Intelligent' means having or showing intelligence, similar to 'smart'.
7.10	Heavy	'Heavy' is the opposite of 'light'.
7.11	Powerful	'Powerful' means having great power or strength, similar to 'strong'.
7.12	Dry	'Dry' is the opposite of 'wet'.
7.13	Small	'Small' is another word for 'tiny'.
7.14	Empty	'Empty' is the opposite of 'full'.
7.15	Simple	'Simple' means easily done or understood, similar to 'easy'.
7.16	Old	'Old' is the opposite of 'young'.
7.17	Spotless	'Spotless' means completely clean, similar to 'clean'.
7.18	Dull	'Dull' is the opposite of 'bright'.

7.19	Silent	'Silent' means not making or accompanied by any sound, similar to 'quiet'.
7.20	End	'End' is the opposite of 'begin'.
7.21	Thrilled	'Thrilled' means extremely excited, similar to 'excited'.
7.22	Rough	'Rough' is the opposite of 'smooth'.
7.23	Huge	'Huge' means very big, similar to 'large'.
7.24	Poor	'Poor' is the opposite of 'rich'.
7.25	Hard	'Hard' means requiring a great deal of effort, similar to 'difficult'.
7.26	Cold	'Cold' is the opposite of 'hot'.
7.27	Enjoyable	'Enjoyable' means capable of giving pleasure, similar to 'fun'.
7.28	Hostile	'Hostile' is the opposite of 'friendly'.
7.29	Terrifying	'Terrifying' means causing extreme fear, similar to 'scary'.
7.30	Dull	'Dull' is the opposite of 'sharp'.
7.31	Furious	'Furious' means extremely angry, similar to 'angry'.
7.32	Shallow	'Shallow' is the opposite of 'deep'.
7.33	Intelligent	'Intelligent' means having or showing intelligence, similar to 'clever'.
7.34	Far	'Far' is the opposite of 'near'.
7.35	Delicious	'Delicious' means highly pleasant to the taste, similar to 'tasty'.
7.36	Dangerous	'Dangerous' is the opposite of 'safe'.
7.37	Miserable	'Miserable' means very unhappy or uncomfortable, similar to 'sad'.
7.38	Shut	'Shut' is the opposite of 'open'.
7.39	Slothful	'Slothful' means lazy and unwilling to work, similar to 'lazy'.
7.40	Low	'Low' is the opposite of 'high'.

Topic 8 – Understanding Mood

In a quiet village, a gentle stream flowed through a lush green meadow. Birds chirped happily in the trees, and a soft breeze rustled the leaves. On the bank of the stream, a group of children laughed as they played. The sun shone warmly, creating a peaceful atmosphere. Butterflies danced in the air, and rabbits hopped in the grass. The children picked flowers and made daisy chains, smiling and chatting. The village was a serene place, where everyone felt calm and joyful.

8.1) What mood is created?

☐ Scary

☐ Exciting

☐ Peaceful

☐ Angry

8.2) How do the children in the story feel?

☐ Frightened

☐ Sad

☐ Happy

☐ Bored

8.3) What makes the village seem serene?

☐ The dark night

☐ The loud noises

☐ The gentle stream

☐ The fast cars

8.4) Which word best describes the atmosphere in?

☐ Chaotic

☐ Peaceful

☐ Gloomy

☐ Noisy

8.5) How do the butterflies and rabbits contribute to the story's mood?

☐ They make it scary

☐ They add to the happiness

☐ They create suspense

☐ They cause confusion

The night was dark and stormy, with thunder rumbling in the distance. In an old, creaky house, shadows flickered as the wind howled outside. A cat hissed at a sudden flash of lightning, and an owl hooted from a nearby tree. Inside the house, an eerie silence filled the empty rooms. Every now and then, a gust of wind would shake the windows. Old portraits on the walls seemed to watch with somber eyes. It was a night full of mystery and suspense, making anyone feel tense and anxious.

8.6) What mood is created?

☐ Cheerful

☐ Mysterious

☐ Calm

☐ Joyful

8.7) What effect does the storm have on the mood?

☐ Makes it sunny

☐ Makes it peaceful

☐ Makes it tense

☐ Makes it happy

8.8) How does the setting of the old house contribute to the mood?

☐ It makes it feel safe

☐ It adds to the eeriness

☐ It makes it feel cozy

☐ It makes it feel modern

8.9) What feeling do the portraits on the walls evoke?

☐ Happiness

☐ Fear

☐ Curiosity

☐ Boredom

8.10) Which word best describes the night?

☐ Lively

☐ Quiet

☐ Stormy

☐ Bright

A festive carnival was in full swing in the heart of the city. Bright lights adorned the rides, and joyful music filled the air. Children's laughter echoed as they eagerly hopped from one ride to another. Vendors sold delicious treats, from cotton candy to hot dogs. Clowns juggled and made balloon animals, adding to the excitement. Families and friends shared moments of joy, capturing pictures as memories. The carnival was a lively celebration, full of fun and happiness.

8.11) What mood is created?

☐ Gloomy

☐ Festive

☐ Scary

☐ Sad

8.12) How do the bright lights contribute to the mood?

☐ Make it sad

☐ Make it joyful

☐ Make it scary

☐ Make it dull

8.13) What feeling does the children's laughter evoke?

☐ Fear

☐ Joy

☐ Loneliness

☐ Anxiety

8.14) Which word best describes the carnival?

☐ Desolate

☐ Eerie

☐ Joyful

☐ Frightening

8.15) How does the presence of clowns affect the story's mood?

☐ Makes it cold

☐ Adds to the excitement

☐ Creates tension

☐ Makes it scary

A quiet library sat surrounded by a garden of blooming flowers. Inside, rows of books stood neatly on shelves, inviting readers to explore. A gentle hush filled the space, with occasional whispers and the soft turning of pages. Sunlight streamed through the windows, casting a warm, inviting glow. People sat comfortably in corners, lost in the worlds within their books. The library was a tranquil haven, a peaceful escape from the outside world.

8.16) What mood is created?

☐ Joyful

☐ Mysterious

☐ Tranquil

☐ Exciting

8.17) What effect does the garden of flowers have on the mood?

☐ Makes it bright

☐ Makes it spooky

☐ Makes it calm

☐ Makes it lively

8.18) How does the sunlight contribute to the mood?

☐ It adds to the joy

☐ It adds to the eeriness

☐ It makes it peaceful

☐ It creates excitement

8.19) What feeling do the rows of books evoke?

☐ Happiness

☐ Fear

☐ Curiosity

☐ Delight

8.20) Which word best describes the library?

☐ Vibrant

☐ Abandoned

☐ Serene

☐ Noisy

The beach was bright and sunny, with waves gently lapping the shore. Families and friends were enjoying picnics, laughter echoing across the sand. Children built sandcastles, while others played in the water. The sky was clear blue, and seagulls flew overhead. Everyone seemed relaxed and happy, enjoying the beautiful day. The scent of the ocean and the sound of the waves created a calming effect. It was a perfect day for fun in the sun, full of joy and relaxation.

8.21) What mood is created?

☐ Gloomy

☐ Scary

☐ Happy

☐ Tense

8.22) How do people at the beach feel?

☐ Worried

☐ Bored

☐ Calm

☐ Angry

8.23) What makes the beach setting feel relaxing?

☐ The fog

☐ The busy crowds

☐ The gentle waves

☐ The loud noise

8.24) Which word best describes the atmosphere?

☐ Chaotic

☐ Peaceful

☐ Gloomy

☐ Dangerous

8.25) How does the sunny weather contribute to the story's mood?

☐ It makes it cold

☐ It adds to the happiness

☐ It creates suspense

☐ It makes it scary

In a gloomy forest, fog covered the ground, and bare trees stood tall. The air was cold and damp, and the path was overgrown. An old, abandoned cabin sat at the edge of the forest, its windows broken. A raven cawed from a tree branch, adding to the spooky atmosphere. Shadows seemed to move in the corner of your eye. It was a place that felt mysterious and slightly unnerving. The forest held secrets, and few dared to explore its depths.

8.26) What mood is created?

☐ Cheerful

☐ Eerie

☐ Calm

☐ Exciting

8.27) What effect does the fog have on the mood?

☐ Makes it sunny

☐ Makes it spooky

☐ Makes it tense

☐ Makes it happy

8.28) How does the setting of the forest contribute to the mood?

☐ It makes it feel safe

☐ It adds to the mystery

☐ It makes it feel cozy

☐ It makes it feel modern

8.29) What feeling does the raven evoke?

☐ Happiness

☐ Fear

☐ Curiosity

☐ Boredom

8.30) Which word best describes the forest?

☐ Eerie

☐ Quiet

☐ Stormy

☐ Bright

In a small cozy village, nestled between rolling hills, a fair was taking place. Colorful booths lined the streets, offering games and treats. Children laughed and ran around, while adults chatted amiably. The smell of fresh pastries and popcorn filled the air. In the center of the village, a band played lively music, adding to the festive atmosphere. People danced and sang along, enjoying the sunny day. The village fair was a scene of joy and community, bringing everyone together in celebration.

8.31) What mood is created?

☐ Gloomy

☐ Festive

☐ Scary

☐ Sad

8.32) How do the colorful booths contribute to the mood?

☐ Make it sad

☐ Make it festive

☐ Make it scary

☐ Make it dull

8.33) What feeling does the band's music evoke?

☐ Fear

☐ Joy

☐ Loneliness

☐ Anxiety

8.34) Which word best describes the village fair?

☐ Desolate

☐ Eerie

☐ Joyful

☐ Frightening

8.35) How does the sunny day affect the story's mood?

☐ Makes it cold

☐ Adds to the happiness

☐ Creates tension

☐ Makes it scary

The city was enveloped in a thick fog that obscured the towering buildings. Streets were empty and silent, creating an eerie feeling. Occasional distant sounds echoed through the fog, adding to the sense of isolation. Streetlights cast a dim glow, barely penetrating the mist. The city, usually bustling with life, now seemed like a ghost town. This foggy night created a sense of mystery and solitude, as if the city was lost in time.

8.36) What mood is created in this story?

☐ Joyful

☐ Mysterious

☐ Cheerful

☐ Exciting

8.37) What effect does the thick fog have on the mood?

☐ Makes it bright

☐ Makes it spooky

☐ Makes it cheerful

☐ Makes it lively

8.38) How does the silence contribute to the mood?

☐ It adds to the joy

☐ It adds to the eeriness

☐ It makes it festive

☐ It creates excitement

8.39) What feeling do the empty streets evoke?

☐ Happiness

☐ Fear

☐ Curiosity

☐ Delight

8.40) Which word best describes the city?

☐ Vibrant

☐ Abandoned

☐ Crowded

☐ Noisy

Topic 8 – Answers

Question Number	Answer	Explanation
8.1	Peaceful	The serene village setting creates a peaceful mood.
8.2	Happy	The children laughing indicates they are happy.
8.3	The gentle stream	The stream contributes to the village's serenity.
8.4	Peaceful	The overall atmosphere in Story 1 is peaceful.
8.5	They add to the happiness	Butterflies and rabbits add to the joyful mood.
8.6	Mysterious	The dark, stormy night and old house create a mysterious mood.
8.7	Makes it tense	The storm adds tension and suspense to the mood.
8.8	It adds to the eeriness	The old house's setting contributes to the eerie mood.
8.9	Fear	The portraits evoke a feeling of fear or unease.
8.10	Stormy	The night is characterized as stormy and tense.
8.11	Festive	The carnival setting with lights and music creates a festive mood.
8.12	Make it joyful	Bright lights contribute to the joyful carnival atmosphere.
8.13	Joy	Children's laughter at the carnival evokes joy.
8.14	Joyful	The carnival is described as a lively and joyful event.
8.15	Adds to the excitement	Clowns add to the carnival's exciting and fun mood.
8.16	Tranquil	The library setting with a gentle hush creates tranquility.
8.17	Makes it calm	The garden of flowers adds calmness to the library's mood.
8.18	It makes it peaceful	Sunlight streaming in adds to the peaceful library atmosphere.

8.19	Curiosity	Rows of books in the library evoke a sense of curiosity.
8.20	Serene	The library in Story 10 is described as serene and tranquil.
8.21	Happy	The beach setting with families enjoying creates a happy mood.
8.22	Calm	People at the beach are described as relaxed and joyful.
8.23	The gentle waves	Gentle waves contribute to the relaxing beach setting.
8.24	Peaceful	The atmosphere at the beach in Story 5 is peaceful.
8.25	It adds to the happiness	Sunny weather enhances the happy and relaxed beach mood.
8.26	Eerie	The gloomy forest with fog creates an eerie mood.
8.27	Makes it spooky	Fog in the forest adds to the spooky and eerie mood.
8.28	It adds to the mystery	The forest setting contributes to the mysterious mood.
8.29	Fear	The raven's caw in the spooky forest evokes fear.
8.30	Eerie	The forest in Story 6 is described as eerie and mysterious.
8.31	Festive	The village fair with colorful booths creates a festive mood.
8.32	Make it festive	Colorful booths at the fair contribute to the festive atmosphere.
8.33	Joy	The band's music at the fair evokes joy and celebration.
8.34	Joyful	The village fair is described as joyful and communal.
8.35	Adds to the happiness	A sunny day enhances the joyful mood of the village fair.
8.36	Mysterious	The foggy city setting creates a mysterious mood.
8.37	Makes it spooky	Thick fog contributes to the spooky city atmosphere.
8.38	It adds to the eeriness	Silence in the foggy city adds to the eerie mood.
8.39	Fear	Empty streets in the foggy city evoke a feeling of isolation and fear.
8.40	Abandoned	The city enveloped in fog and described as silent seems abandoned.

Ready for More?

The NWEA MAP testing is adaptive. This means that if your student found these questions too tricky or too easy, they may find it useful to practice grades below or above they grade they are in. This will expose students to new concepts and ideas, giving them a better chance at scoring higher in tests.

Alexander-Grace Education produces books covering Mathematics, Sciences, and English, to help your student maximize their potential in these areas.

For errata, please email
alexandergraceeducation@gmail.com

Made in the USA
Monee, IL
06 May 2025